# Final Steps In
# Christian Maturity

by
Jeanne Guyon

*Final Steps in Christian Maturity*
Copyrighted by SeedSowers Publishing House
Printed in the United States of America
All rights reserved

Published by The SeedSowers
           P.O.Box 285, Sargent, GA 30275
           1-800-228-2665

Cover design by David Smith

---

Library of Congress Cataloging-in-Publication Data

Guyon, Jeanne
           Final Steps in Christian Maturity / Jeanne Guyon
           ISBN 0-940232-22-7
           1. Spiritual Life.   1. Title

---

Times New Roman 12pt

*Formerly entitled*

# The Spiritual Adventure

Taken from excerpts of a larger,
three-volume work entitled

# Justifications

These excerpts first published in English
privately by
George W. McCall in 1915

# EDITOR'S PREFACE

Louise XIV ordered Jeanne Guyon to the city of Meaux, there to appear before Arch-Bishop Bossuet (who was perhaps the best known churchman of all Europe) and two other well-known Roman Catholic bishops. Mme. Guyon was to spend several days being grilled by these three men on the subject of her teachings.

There were two possible accusations which they might charge her with: one called "heresy," and a lesser (but still very serious charge) called "novel opinions." Jeanne Guyon was not one to walk away from what she considered to be a misunderstanding of her teachings. She faced these three men in full confidence that she would be vindicated — perhaps even commended — *not* condemned! Unfortunately, it was not to turn out so favorably.

These three men took her autobiography, a book called *Method Of Prayer* (now under the title of *Experiencing the*

*Depths of Jesus Christ*), and her commentary on the *Song of Songs* and used them as the evidence whereby they would decide her fate.

Wisely or unwisely, Guyon decided to assist these churchmen in making their decision by presenting—in writing—a full explanation of her teachings. During a period of fifty days she wrote a treatise that—when published—was three huge volumes of some 400 pages *each*, entitled *The Justifications*. As far as we know, this three-volume work was printed in French only, and one time only. To our knowledge, there has never been a publication of this work in English. The only French editions still in existence, if there are any, probably exist in some musty vaults somewhere in France. A smaller English edition of those three volumes—excerpts, if you please—did appear in 1915. You now hold in your hand a *modern* edition of that small condensation.

Whoever selected these excerpts obviously picked out the very best passages, because what we have here is Mme. Guyon at her finest!

What are the *Justifications*?

Guyon took extracts of writings of the *Saints* of the past—people whom the Roman Catholic Church had given its blessing—and then compared those teachings with her own. She was proving she had "justification" for her teachings and the terminology she used. She went even so far as to say that these saints, authorities and authors of bygone days had used stronger expressions and been more emphatic in their teachings than she! Her efforts were all to naught. It is doubtful these men even glanced at her *Justifications*!

What did happen? For a long time, nothing! Guyon spent nearly six months in a convent in Meaux, directly under Bossuet's supervision. Eventually he released her. When the king found this out, he went into a rage at the very thought of this strange woman's being loose again in the world. Louis immediately ordered her arrest and imprisonment. The rest is history.

*Justifications* has been largely overlooked and/or neglected through the centuries. A modern rewrite of these available excerpts seems to indicate that *Justifications* might be among her best works. Or did the translator simply glean the best out of 1200 pages, giving the cream to us in this 10 percent?

One thing is obvious, someone selected these excerpts with great care. The modern Christian would do well to read, re-read, and reflect on the contents of this small but remarkable book.

**There are many willing to bear the cross; almost none . . . the infamy.**

**JEANNE GUYON**

# 1
# WHAT IS THE MOST COURAGEOUS OF ALL ABANDONMENTS?

How far are you willing to go in yielding your will to God? How far is proper? What are the limits of obedience, the ends of abandonment, the ultimate willingness of the will? The *Song of Songs*, Chapter 5, records a possible insight, for there you find a soul giving up *the hope* of *eternal life*!

This does not mean that this particular believer had eternal life taken from him! It simply means that this believer offered up to God even *that* hope. There was now *nothing* but a present love for God. All hope *of any personal reward* for loving God was abandoned and sacrificed.

---

Editors note:
    This chapter of *Final Steps in Christian Maturity* is an excerpt taken from the original French edition, Volume I, page 9.

From a human and earthly viewpoint, this believer looks as though he were in the hands of the raging enemy, and it appears that God has abandoned him. This believer may even *think* himself lost. Certainly it is clear that he has relinquished his hope of salvation.

Here, then, you see a true and *great* sacrifice, a monumental yielding of a soul abandoning itself to God. We do have an illustration here of a sacrifice that is *pure*. The motive behind the sacrifice is love, even *excessive* love. This sacrifice is accompanied by an abandonment of every selfish interest. This believer, we discover, prefers hell to sin! (Paradoxically, he may still *feel* that he is committing some terrible sin. The pain can be very deep. This pain is present because he has a deep sensitivity to having offended God. He may even feel it necessary to cry out, "Destroy me, Oh Lord, but allow me not to sin.")

Other Christians may fear hell because hell is a punishment for sin, but here is a soul who demands to be sent to hell *rather than* to sin willfully against his God. (Later in his spiritual growth, this sense of unworthiness before the Lord will diminish; it diminishes as a result of *resignation*, patience and quiet.)

Let us take this high water mark, this extreme view of yielding and abandon, and hold it before our eyes as we venture into the interior of life.

# 2
# THE BLESSEDNESS OF WINTER!

I see the season of *winter* as an excellent example of the transforming work of the Lord in a Christian's life. When winter comes, the vegetable world, it seems to me, reflects the image of the purifying which God does in order to remove imperfections from the life of one of his children.

As cold comes on the wings of a winter storm, the trees gradually begin to lose their leaves. The green is soon changed into a funereal brown; soon the leaves fall away and die. Behold the tree's appearance now! It looks stripped and desolate. Behold the loss of summer's beautiful garment. What happens as you look upon that poor tree? You see a revelation.

Under all the beautiful leaves there had been all sorts of irregularities and defects. The defects had been invisible because of the beautiful leaves. Now those defects are startlingly revealed! The tree is no longer beautiful in its surface appearance. But has the tree actually changed? Not at all. Everything is *exactly* as it was before. Everything is as it has *always* been! It is just that the leaves are no longer there to *hide* what is *real*. The beauty of the outward life of the leaves had only hidden what had always been present.

The same is true of you. The same is true of all believers. We can each look so beautiful . . . until life disappears! Then, no matter who, the Christian is revealed as full of defects. As the Lord works on you to produce purification, you will appear stripped of all your virtues! But, in the tree, there *is* life inside; and, as the tree, you are not actually becoming worse, you are simply seeing yourself for what you really are! Know that somewhere deep within the tree of winter there is still the life that produced last spring's beautiful leaves.

No, the believer's *inmost being* has not been deprived of its essential virtue. He has lost no advantages. He has only lost something human, *a sense of his own personal goodness*, and he has discovered, instead, his utter wretchedness. He has lost the *ease* of following the Lord. That ease was born more of ignorance of self than anything else.

As with the tree, so with you.

The Christian, now spoiled and naked, appears in his own eyes to be a denuded thing; and all those around him see his defects *for the first time*: defects which were previously veiled, concealed by outward graces.

Sometimes such revelation is so devasting to the pride of a Christian he simply never recovers, and decides to be a Christian on some other level; or gives up following the Lord entirely.

Throughout the long cold winter, the tree certainly appears as dead as the very deadest of all trees in the forest. The tree knows no reality. Here is *total* destruction, it seems. But the truth lies somewhere else.

That tree is actually undergoing and sumitting to a process which *preserves* its life and *strengthens* the tree! After all, what does winter do to a tree? It contracts the tree's exterior. The life deep within is no longer uselessly expended! Its life, rather, is concentrated within the deepest part of the trunk and in the hidden portions of the root. The life is forced deeper and deeper into the inmost part of the tree.

Winter preserves the tree, no matter how dead the tree may appear. Yes, its leaves have fallen away and its true, deformed, state has been exposed; yet the tree has never been more alive than at that time! During the winter, the source and principle of life is more firmly established *than in any other season*.

In all the other seasons, the tree employs the whole force of its life in adorning and beautifying itself. But it does so at the *expense* of expending its life, taking its very vitality from the roots and the deepest part of the trunk. There must be winter. Winter is necessary for the tree if it is to live, survive and flourish.

Virtue has a way of sinking deep within the Christian, while totally *disappearing* from the surface, leaving the outward and natural defects in *very* conspicuous view!

If we have eyes to see, then we see that this is beautiful.

Grace operates in your life in exactly the same way. God will take away the leaves. *Something* will cause them to fall. The outward virtue will collapse. He does this that he may strengthen the *principle* of the virtue. The source of virtue must be built up. Something deep within the soul is still functioning. Somewhere within the spirit the functions that are the highest (in God's estimation) have never rested. What is going on is exceedingly hidden. It is humble.

What is happening is *pure* love.

What is going on in the inmost part is absolute abandonment and contempt of self. The inward man is making progress. The soul is venturing forth into the interior. True, it seems that the operations of God are concentrated on the external parts of the believer, and even a moment's glance reveals that the exterior things are not pleasant to look upon. Yet, in truth, *no new defects* in the soul have developed! Only the uncovering of old faults has come about! And, as they are exposed, they are better healed.

If you dare the spiritual pilgrimage, you need to remember in times of calamity, and in times of what appear to be dry spells, and in that time which men will call *a spiritual winter*: Life is there.

If winter comes . . .

Vol. II
Page 265

# 3

# IN QUIET

One of the first things a spiritual pilgrim must learn is to be quiet before God *and to remain* before Him — coming without any request or even any personal will in *any* matter.

If the believer chooses to act on his own he is, of course, hindering the progress of God. He is being active strictly for his own activity's sake. (He has chosen to do something *for* God rather than *by* God.) As he begins to come before the Lord, it is better for the believer to learn to die to all influences of motivation that originate in the self, which — after all — only aggrandize his self nature. If one remains before the Lord without will, he becomes like soft wax, a perfectly manageable instrument in the hands of God.

Now the believer passes into a new state, that of being

active, *yet* having a will that is yielded up, with no motive of its own. The believer's actions are no longer self-originating, they come from those gentle and loving influences of an indwelling Holy Spirit within his bosom.

Vol. I, page 114.

# 4

# OUR DESIRE,
# FROM SELF OR FROM GOD?

Let us now see a person who has surrendered his life to his Lord. I find it impossible to believe that one who places his whole happiness, his whole state, in the hands of God alone could then continue to have a list of desires for his own happiness to bring to his Lord. None but that one who dwells in God *by love* can place all his happiness in God alone. To seek to place your happiness in God by the strength of your will, or out of fear, or even "to please God" are all horrible states and poor motives.

Love alone should cause anyone to yield up his will to the Lord. If it is not love that produces submission, eventually that submission will come out as something *brutish*. When the believer relinquishes his soul, his will, his all to his Lord, desires nothing of himself and desires only God for the sake of God (and that, in a state of passionate love), then we see that he has made a good beginning. Why? Because *here* is a state where there is no enjoyment with self *as an end* in view!

The glory of heaven is not the motive. Nor can the motive be the wonderful feeling of the Lord's presence. There must be *no object*, earthly or heavenly, that is your ultimate desire. It is only that you have loved Him, have fallen in love with Him, and are in a state of loving Him.

It has been wisely said, "Motive is but the child of love." If I love God alone, I will desire God alone. If I love God alone for Himself alone, with no thought of self, then my desire will be in Him alone. Later, to be sure, whatever comes from *within* will be pure and without selfish motive.

There is no dominance of "vivaciousness" in this desire of love. Rather there is an element of quietness and rest. Pure motive and pure desire are quiet and restful, filled and satisfied. If a love is expressed toward an infinite God, and if that love itself has its origins in Him, and if the believer has no goal but the blessedness of God, then the desires within the heart of that believer could not be manifested in something as common as restlessness or unsatisfied wants. There must be present a sense of rest, a sense that "I have no ungratified wish, no unfullfilled personal desire."

Please realize that *this* foundation alone can be the true foundation—and the only unshakable foundation—for the believer to build his spiritual life upon. Be mindful that most believers love God with some other state than this *mixed in*. There is a love for God that has within it a regard for the self and its needs. Even worse, and perhaps more common, is the believer whose love for God is actually a love (and a seeking) for the gratification of his own being. He is seeking God because of what *he feels* when he loves his Lord. When *that* love dies (that is, when the feeling that goes along with that love dies), this Christian loses a great deal of interest in God!

This is a self-seeking state, and it must be abandoned if we are to know true spiritual growth. We must love Him without any end in view and even — as must come — without *any feeling* present to buttress us! We must love Him with total disregard to dry spells *and* to times of spiritual abundance. Our love must pass beyond the gratification that we get in loving God . . . otherwise we are built on sifting sand.

It is true that *God* may plant desires within you. *He* does plant motives within the heart of a believer. Paul had such a thing happen to him when he cried out, "I am in a straight between two alternatives. I desire to depart and be with Christ, which is far better, and yet I also need to be here with you."

But remember, this is the same Paul who could cry out under the influence of his love in Christ for his Hebrew brothers, "I would that I could be cut off from Christ for the sake of my brothers." (He cried out these words with a love that had been put into him by his God.) When he cried out these words it was *also* with an absolute freedom from any personal considerations. Self was not there! Here Paul expresses contradictory feelings, and yet they are perfectly reconciled in the depths of the human spirit. There is some-

**11**

thing going on there in the depths of the spirit which never changes.

The only happiness and interest of the believer is in the blessedness of God, for God, and in God. All perceivable desires of that believer have merged with, and been swallowed up in, the desire for God. Nonetheless, there is deposited within him a desire which originates in God, a desire which is best for God and for His Kingdom.

There is a far distance between the day when a believer comes to the Lord in this manner and an earlier day when this same believer sat in the seat of selfishness when he came before his Lord.

The desire that is born within the self, that has reference to the self, is the result of a will that is still unpurified. It is your Lord's desire to bring that will to nothing . . . until the will is one with your Lord. Therefore your Lord must, from time to time, absorb — yes, and destroy — self-originating desires.

By what evidence can you know you are in this state of self originating desires and not in a will which is in concert with God? Ah, the answer is simple and is really *quite easy* to discern! A believer who has been persecuted and becomes bitter . . . a believer who has known disappointment because of the conduct of another believer (or someone in the world) and is resentful . . . and most of all, *that Christian who has been disappointed in God* because of what *He* has done, and is unhappy with God and with the state he is in at the hands of so unfair a God . . . surely a Christian who experiences these emotions is *not* in a state where his will is in concert with God; he is, rather, in a state where self is originating the desires of the heart.

We do not always understand the will of God, but to trust His sovereignty completely is another matter.

When the Christian fixes his mind *on what God should be*, and then when God does not act according to his expectation, he will surely suffer disappointment. Further, be sure, he has not a soul abandoned to the providence of God! He is not seeking the felicity and the well-being of God alone. There is a mixture. *That mixture* can destroy his inner walk with the Lord.

As the believer deepens in his abandonment to Christ, *outward things* (caused by persecution, injustice, and even what is perceived to be the unfairness of God and the displeasure of God) are things no longer perceived nor reacted to.

Volume I
Page 180

# 5

# HIS WILL YOURS

How is it that the Lord plants *His* desire within the bosom of the believer?

There comes a point in the Lord's dealing when He desires to give a believer some spiritual blessing, some experience, or perhaps even some material thing.

At this point, we must understand the way of prayer. The Lord prepares the heart of the believer to receive the blessing, then He gives that believer the desire which blossoms forth from within the heart. (Psalm 37:4) How does the Lord do this?

The Spirit of God, who dwells in you, begins to make intercession in you; and that intercession is *for* you . . . and it is according to the will of God. *He* intercedes and *He* requests (from *within* you) the very thing which is the desire of His heart! Now it is no longer only the desire of God and the Spirit, it also has become the desire within the bosom of the believer.

The request actually comes from the Holy Spirit, the desire actually comes from the Father. The believer's will only becomes one with that desire.

The desire for *humiliation* on the part of the believer is a state far beneath the desire of the believer to *love* God; and yet sometimes it pleases God to humble the Christian (perhaps by means of slander); therefore, the Lord infuses into the Christian a great thirst for humiliations. I call this "*the thirst.*" (I deliberately used the word "thirst" here to distinguish it from the word "desire."

There are other times when the Lord will *incline* the believer to pray for particular things. The believer is perfectly aware that this prayer does not originate within his own will. Rather, the prayer and the desire have originated *in God.* The believer is not free to pray for *whom* he pleases, for *what* he pleases, or even *when* he pleases!

In this better way of prayer, the Christian is never vaulted up nor proud, nor does he have self congratulations when this prayer is specifically answered. He knows perfectly well that it was the Lord who first possessed that desire, that it was the Lord who prayed it, and that it was the Lord within him who granted *His own* petition!

All this seems to me infinitely more clear in my own mind than I can make it on this paper.

Vol. I
Page 180

# 6

# THE POWER OF SIMPLICITY

The purer an element is, the simpler the structure of that element. It follows, therefore, that the more extended is the selflessness of that element, the more ways it can be used. Let me illustrate.

Nothing can be purer nor simpler than water. Certainly nothing on all this earth has a greater range of uses. Why? Because of its fluidity. It has no sensible qualities of its own. It is ready to receive all sorts of impressions and be contented. It is tasteless in itself but can carry an infinite variety of tastes. It is not correct to say that water in itself possesses qualities of color and scent. These qualities are impressed upon the water *by that which is put within* the water! It is the very capacity *to be free from taste and color*, to be *pure*, to be *simple* that allows water to exhibit such a great variety and abundance of applications!

If you ask water, "What are your properties?" the water will reply, "My properties are to have no property at all. I am inert." "But," you may reply, "I see you have a red color." "I dare say," the water will answer, "but I, nonetheless, am not red by nature, *nor do I question* what is done with me, either in imparting to me flavor or color."

Furthermore, water treats *form* the same way it treats *color*. It is fluid and yielding. It instantly and exactly assumes the form of the vessel in which it is placed. If water had consistency and properties which it firmly held on to, it would not be able to take every form that it is called upon to yield to . . . just as it would not be able to give the appearance of every tint and hue.

So it is also with the indwelling Holy Spirit; so it is *also* with the human *will* . . . when the will is in a state of simplicity and purity. Water has no flavor nor color derived from its own self. Just as water owes its scent or tint to what dwells within it, so it is with *the human will* abandoned *to God*! God is the author of whatever is manifest.

I see *this* to be the proper state of the believer's will. The soul no longer distinguishes or takes knowledge of anything of itself; the will sees nothing as belonging to itself. *There* is its purity. Everything that comes to it from the Lord, it receives. *Nor does it withhold any part for its own self.*

What personal loss that is! But behold the gain! What loss there would be to all if there were not this loss! How much water teaches us!

# 7

# THE PATH TOO OFTEN FOLLOWED

One who is enjoying God in an unspeakable degree has acquired a very refined taste and is not easily pleased by earthly things. He who has known this high state and who *then* leaves his Lord and permits himself to be guilty of offenses against Him is one *who sought Him only for His delights* and His goodness. He did not seek Him for Himself *alone.*

When the Lord takes things away, when He allows harshness, when things seem unjust, then invariably this "seeking one" will leave and find his pleasure elsewhere. When God no longer pleases him, he looks to the world, to other people, perhaps even to other believers, to please himself. But mark this: *His state has not really ever changed!* He is simply looking for that which will make him happy! *That* is his *constant* state. He cares for himself, for what makes him feel nice inside. This is, of course, nothing more than self-gratification, using things spiritual to obtain that gratification.

Almost every soul who suffers will find himself seeking too much comfort! He will be *too eager* to get out from under his suffering. Rather than being willing to die, he is looking for a way out.

When the believer arrives at this point, one of two things will usually happen: He will either turn back, seeking his former activities, seeking — in them — to recover from the suffering and pain, seeking to enjoy that which was lost . . . seeking comfort. Or perhaps (which is far worse) discovering he has no sense or feeling of God, he will find sense and feelings somewhere else.

I have stated before that such love for God is impure and it is sensual, entirely selfish. When there are no longer delights in God in which to be indulged, such a soul will begin to slip away from God. Satisfying the senses with spiritual experience is *not* a spiritual walk!

Francis De Sales stated, "The moment their pleasures in God cease, they turn to those pleasures which are unlawful. If their taste has been refined by their participation in spiritual enjoyment, they cannot now be satisfied with other things, except by an infinite and unceasing amount of inordinate pleasure."

Such ones are seeking to stifle the conscience (and perhaps their remorse) by a very unbridled license. Had they loved God with an affection that was completely pure they would not have fallen at the time when they entered into sufferings.

In truth, this introduction to *great* pain is the most dangerous period of one's whole spiritual life. When the Lord takes away interior support, the soul of the believer will invariably desire to turn to external sources for pleasure and comfort, and to *once more* have delights. As time passes, it becomes clear that *he is seeking for a way out* of this uncomfortable state. Many a spiritual pilgrim has been destroyed here.

This is a matter that I have consistently pointed out in my writings.

Certainly, in the beginning, and from time to time thereafter, the Lord draws us with great delights and with much heavenly comfort. He draws us with something that is strong and powerful, sometimes even overwhelming. But since the injustices, sufferings and pain of life so often distract a believer, we make a most significant discovery: *The blessings of God are not really strong at all.* The memory of the most wonderful heavenly delights *ever known* can quickly vanish from memory in the face of injustice, persecution, suffering and pain! This is why it is so important, when the Christian begins to encounter sufferings in his life, that he not run from those sufferings, but accept them. More, that he not seek to be relieved of them, nor to have them ended by embracing comforts and delights.

The believer must come to a point when he is no longer *blown about* by these winds. Later, he must not be *subject* to frailties. He must come to a place where he does not stumble in the hour when he must live in less than heavenly delight. (Yet, this state must not be simply an exercise of a strong human will.)

To live out your life in less than heavenly delight is to be expected. These things *do* happen to believers! Furthermore, the loss of heavenly delights is often accomplished by what John Of the Cross called the *night of the senses—* when the senses begin to fall into a dark night. The *sense* of the spiritual disappears! Yes, this is a very frightening thing for the believer, but it need not be so if he perseveres through this time and does not seek a way out.

A believer who seeks God for God alone may often *appear* to be one who has been *abandoned* rather than gratified! However he is *not* abandoned by God. Sometimes this believer will even *realize* that it is better to fear blessing than to receive it! And he will love the cross without fearing that instrument at all.

There is a place which can be reached by the soul that might be referred to as total death. The soul of the believer becomes so confirmed in God that it can find nothing satisfying in all creation. To leave God, after coming to this state, would render that soul the most miserable thing in the universe. Why? Because he knows that he will never derive any pleasure from exterior sources. All else appears insipid in comparison to celestial delights. To feast on outward things would only double the torture.

What agonies Lucifer must have suffered when, having been thrown out of the riches of heaven, he had to dwell in the realms of earth, nor could he go back to heavenly delights. The more advanced Christian seems to sense that if he does not follow on with the Lord, his own state might be similar; therefore, he dare not fall. This is a Christian who is resting in God, who does not need *delight* (nor the rescue provided by external comforts) in order to follow his Lord.

Again, this is why I say it is difficult for a more advanced believer to fall away. He sees the end result of what will take place in his life. Little by little, he is settled into a fixed state. Eventually, it will take pride and maliciousness of *purpose* to move him from his relationship with the Lord. It *is* possible for him to fall, of course, just as it was possible for the rebellious angels to do so; but see how difficult it was for them to *return* to God. I would say the difficulty of falling and the difficulty of returning are about equal. Falling away *and* returning both come very close to being impossible. In all situations we face, the Lord furnishes every one of us with means of salvation; but on account of the wickedness of such a departure, repentence would be difficult. And if I may speak after the manner of men, I would say that a loss of this kind must be more painful to God than that of a million others.

But let us return our concentration to those who are *just entering* the interior way, and who may experience a "night of their senses." Such souls are not firmly established in God. There has been no experiencing of the death to self (though it was accomplished on the cross of Christ). When they find that they are no longer experiencing the delights which they originally found *in first knowing* God, they turn to enjoyments which are *not found* in God. However, the worldly pleasures, they discover, are blunted; therefore, they must run in excess to find emotions that will satisfy them. It is a miracle when such ones turn again to God, for when they have once tasted the good things, the heavenly things of God, and then have abandoned them, return is difficult.

# 8

# GOD CANNOT BE FOUND
# OUTSIDE OF HIMSELF

The question is often asked me, "Should not the novice, a beginner in the inward way, seek the Lord outwardly first, and move from there to seeking Him within?"

A spiritual beginning is not a beginning when it seeks Him in a roundabout way! To consider such a proposition is a great mistake. If a young believer seeks God externally, he will be looking for a God who is *distinct* and *separate*. This is a tragedy, for he will search from one end of heaven to the other for his Lord.

And what will be the result? This young believer, instead of becoming internal in his Christian walk and collecting all of his being in the presence of God and calling on his Lord from his internal being — instead of doing that, he will dissipate and waste his strength in looking for his Lord in a place *where He is not.*

You are familiar with the principles by which an artist works to obtain the proper lines within his painting. He brings in certain lines, coming from scattered and many places on the canvas, moving the scene toward a central place within the picture. Each line becomes stronger as it nears another; the lines move toward some central point, somewhere within the center of the canvas. Counterwise, each line becomes feeble and indistinct as it recedes from that center. So it is with the believer.

The believer turns *within* to his spirit, and the Lord comes and joins him *there* — in the *realm* of the spirit. The more this occurs, the greater is the drawing to God; and the more is appropriated to that believer the power of performing *His* work.

Again, as you look at a painting, you see the lines widely scattered, but gradually coming to unite in a central place. So the soul, coming from many scattered and different places, centers in one particular place where nothing is divided and nothing is divisible. It is at *that point* that the soul has the ability, yes, the power, of finding God.

If a Christian is to become interior and is to become spiritual, he must begin by seeking God *within* . . . by collecting together all of his thoughts. Unless he does that, he will never reach that central place where God dwells. But once he has arrived there, he must *depart* again (not by returning to the many external places but *by passing through* and *beyond* himself) and go *even further* inward toward the *center* of his God. This is the true going forth *from* himself. The believer departs from himself *not* by going *outward*, *away* from himself, but by going *inward*, *away* from himself. It is not the collecting together of thoughts and the whole being, but it is, having done that, to move further beyond one's self (the center of the creature) into the center of the Creator.

Think of the center of the soul as a sort of halfway house, or an *inn*. The traveler must necessarily pass by that inn at some point on his/her journey. When he has stayed at the inn a while and is prepared to depart, he does not retrace his steps, but goes onward up the high road. The further he goes beyond that inn, the further he also leaves self behind, both in sight and in sensual (outward) feelings. As one moves toward the center of his being, *there* he will find God. He is invited to come forth from himself and pass further in.

When we reach that point, *then* it is that we pass into our Lord. It is here, at the center of our being, that we meet Him. *Beyond even that point* we *truly* find Him in the place where self no longer is. The further we journey, the further we advance toward Him, the further we depart from self.

# 9

# FROM SELF TO GOD

A Christian's progress into God should be measured by his separation from self.

How do I define self? It is the individual's views, his feelings, the things which he remembers and thinks about, his own personal self-interests and self-reflections. This is self. When a believer first comes into the presence of his Lord and begins advancing toward the center of his being, he will be very much absorbed in self-reflection and will be very aware of himself. The nearer he comes to the center of his being, where he will meet his Lord, he is *even more* absorbed with himself!

When, however, he has actually arrived at the center of his being, he ceases looking upon himself. His feelings, his remembrances, his self-interests and self-reflections become less and less. In proportion to his passing away from — and beyond — himself, he sees less and less of himself because his face is turned, not toward himself, but in another direction.

Self reflection *is* helpful and important in the beginning; but *at this point* would not be helpful, but *injurious*.

When one sets out to move in the inward way, be sure that his views will, necessarily, be self-directed and they will be complex. This is as it should be. But they *will eventually become* simple and more centered in the spirit (yet without ceasing to have self-direction). Later the soul is still directed, but it is not centered on itself. At this point the soul is gifted with a single eye.

Once again I will speak of the inn. As the traveler approaches a halfway house and as that house comes into full view, he has no need to look for directions or wonder where he is. He can fix his eye on the first goal of his journey, the inn which is before him. Now as he enters into the inn, he no longer has to think of the passage to the inn nor of the inn itself. He has come to a place of rest. He has arrived at the center. The problems of the journey, and arriving at the inn, are behind him.

The Christian learns to pass beyond *even this point* to a place where self-perception *almost* ceases, and there is only a perception of God, of being with God, of being in God, and perhaps even being lost in God. There is less and less a concentration upon self and more of being lost in God. I would even say "lost in the abyss of God." He may even reach that place where he no longer knows nor discerns anything but his Lord. (It goes without saying that

30

any personal reflection would be at this time harmful to his fellowship with God.)

Now we must ask, "By what means does one pass beyond self?" The answer is, by means of the surrender of the will. And what do I mean by the surrender of the will?

The will is the ruler of our understanding and our memory. Those two may be distinctly separated, yet they are definitely one. When one has come to the center of his being (when he has come to that halfway house) his *understanding* and his *memory* have been surrendered over to God.

(These two elements are to be surrendered over to God, not to anything else, but to God. Not to self, not to others, but to *Him*.)

A person who has passed beyond this point (the leaving of self, the surrender of his will) is—in his function— almost a wholly different person from the one who started out striving to reach the center of his being.

Now I would say to the believer who is seeking after God that he must go beyond this point.

If one is to be established *firmly* in God, he must put a great distance beyond this point. The inward parts of a man are not easily changed and converted. You see, on arrival at this halfway house, *one* penetration into the depths of God changes us not at all. If we are truly to be converted, we must continually endeavor to recollect ourselves in our center.

Therefore I would *never* pause or dwell on *anything* which has been said in this book thus far! One should not be taught (and one should not teach) over and over what has been said up until now. This would be like asking the food in the stomach to return to the mouth again! That would be the forerunner of death. No, the halfway house is still only *introductory*. Do not remain here. And if you teach the interior way and can bring others *only* to here, you have accomplished little, if anything!

Having learned to come to the halfway house, the Christian must now explore areas beyond that. He must do so frequently and continually.

We are only gradually converted!

# 10

# THE TRUE BEGINNING
# OF THIS ADVENTURE

When a Christian has first taken the inward way, he
will find many difficulties in applying the illustration of the
halfway house from the previous chapter. But when he has
ventured *beyond* that point and left behind the wandering
mind, the many thoughts, and begun his first experience of
a oneness with God, he will find much joy and much
delight. He may also make a great mistake, saying, "Here,
at last, is the Christian life." Nothing could be further from
the truth. In this period of the Christian's life, the Lord
draws him with joys, with spiritual senses, with many
graces. Truly, this is a wonderful and memorable time in a
believer's life. But the true adventure lies ahead, and so does
the test.

Not many Christians seek after a deeper walk with

their Lord. Not many even try to find the halfway house; and many who do, get discouraged. Those few who travel on — and begin to touch a oneness with Christ and are refreshed by many spiritual graces and wonderful discoveries — will, nonetheless, *very* often fall away at that later time when enthusiasm has died down and when they have become used to spiritual encounter. The "new" wears off as they grow older in years.

There comes a time in the believer's life when the Lord withdraws the joy. He will seemingly withdraw the graces. At the same time, the Christian may also find himself in a period of persecution — persecution, no less, than that coming from Christians in religious authority. Further, he may find much difficulty in his home or private life. He may also be experiencing great difficulties with his health. *Somewhere* there will be a great deal of pain or other losses too numerous to mention. The believer may also be undergoing experiences which he feels are totally unique to himself. Other Christians, in whom he has put his trust, may forsake him and mistreat him. He may feel that he has been very unjustly treated. He will feel this toward men and he will feel it toward his God, for — in the midst of all this other pain and confusion — it will seem that God, too, has left him!

Even more believers give up the journey when the Lord seems to have forsaken them in the spirit and left their spirit dead — while the world and all else is crashing in on them, friends forsaking them, and great suffering and pain abounding everywhere in their lives.

34

*Now* comes the true test of discipleship. It is only *here* that our commitment to Christ is tested. There has been adventure, enthusiasm, and the excitement of launching out into the unknown, as well as the joy of finding a deep fellowship with God. But the true land of promise *always* lies beyond a vast wasteland. Promise is found only on the far side of a desert.

When a Christian has reached this wilderness, this desolate place, this dark night of the senses, this time that touches the very experience of Christ when He cried out "Why??" . . . it is only at *that* time, when the believer walks by naked faith, that he begins to become truly established and well founded in his Lord.

Only a few will, quietly and serenely, continue to *seek after* Him. Hidden. Humble. Unnoticed. Unrewarded. Unproclaimed. Expecting nothing, except that *God* be blessed! Not the creature! But God!

We only begin (there, within our inmost being,) where we have lost everything . . . yes, even our deeper relationship to Christ!

When you can walk to the halfway house without feeling, without sense; when you can go beyond that place and, *not seeing your Lord*, believe He is there by the eyes of faith alone; when you can walk further and further into Christ when there are no senses, no feelings, not even the slightest registration of the presence of God; when you can sit before Him when everything around you and within you seems to be either falling apart or dead; and when you can come before your Lord without question and without demand, serene in faith *alone*, and there, before Him, worship Him without distraction, without a great deal of consciousness of self, and with no spiritual sense of Him, yet with your whole being centered and turned on Him, then will the test of commitment begin to be established. *Then* will *begin* the true journey of the Christian life.

# 11

# SPIRITUAL ADDICTION, REPUTATION, AND THE CROSS!

The Christian soul must partake of, touch and embrace the Lord's own experiences, which is an enigmatic state. The way of the Christian's soul is but a constant succession of encounters with the eternal cross, with ignominy and confusion.

Many people abandon themselves, quite successfully, to certain encounters with the cross; but refuse to abandon themselves to *all* such encounters. One thing they can *never* prevail on themselves to allow: that their *reputation*, in the sight of men, *be taken away.* And yet it is here, at this point and similar points, where God is aiming. He will bring you even there! And expect of you . . . no bitterness!

Your Lord intends for your soul to *really* die to the ways of the self nature! He sometimes permits an apparent (not a real) mistake to be made, so that your reputation will be destroyed in the eyes of men.

I once knew of a person of the interior way who came upon a number of most terrible crosses. Among them was the loss of her reputation. Her reputation was something to which she was extremely attached. She could not bring herself to give up her reputation. She begged her God that He give her any cross but that; thus she formally *refused* her consent to that cross.

She told me that since that time there has been no spiritual progress in her life. She has remained where she was! So total and so fatal was this reservation to her progress that, since that time, the Lord has never once given her humiliations in the sight of men; *nor*, since that time, has He given her the grace of spiritual progress!

God will sometimes call on a Christian to turn back from the inward and to apply himself to things without. Why? *Because that person has become addicted to an inward retreat.* Many a believer is quite certain that he will never have to bear *this* cross; but if leaving inward solitude is the thing necessary, in order for us to encounter the cross, then that is what the Lord will do. And He really does sometimes separate a Christian from spiritual things which — perhaps unknown to himself — the Christian is addicted to or prideful in. (Yes, it is quite frequent that a Christian becomes prideful about his inward retreat, and *not* know it!)

# 12

# THE SPIRIT'S DARK NIGHT

There is a night, an obscure night, of the spirit. What is this obscure night of the spirit that is referred to by John Of the Cross? It is the Lord's way of purifying.

There comes a point in the spiritual pilgrimage when many of the defects of *the inward man* seem to have disappeared. But they do make their reappearance! Not in the inward man, but on the surface. They reappear in *the outer man*! In this reappearing, they carry stronger features than ever before. I refer to matters of temper, hasty words, action, reaction, rebellious thought, and capricious conduct. The Christian finds he can no longer *easily* practice virtue and good works. *All* of his imperfections seem to reappear!

God lays His hand heavily upon this person. Those around him slander him. He is subject to the most unexpected types of persecutions. His own thoughts become rebellious. It seems he is under seige from Satan himself. But it is in this terrible array of crucifying instruments that the inward man is made to succumb, and yields to death. If any of these elements were missing, then the deep imperfections of the inward man *would* remain.

When I speak of defects, I speak of something that is not voluntary but, rather, things within us of which we are not conscious. Nonetheless, the recent absence of God leads the believer to think that his own faults are the cause of the loss of God's presence.

The believer seems suspended, as it were, at a distance from God. His misery is complete. The Lord seems to thrust this poor soul out the door. (But He does this in His providence.) At this point the believer often finds himself caught up in the commerce of the world. This is *not* where he wishes to be, but it is where he has been placed.

Let us see what is happening. Here is this poor creature discovering, almost hourly, his own defects. He is under the strength of God's strongest hand. He is experiencing his own weaknesses and the malice of men and the opposition of devils. *God is working His purpose.* Those who do not consent to such a crucifying process will remain throughout their lifetime with a defective inward man.

(Sometimes in one stroke the Lord delivers this one from every foe and receives him, purified, back into Himself. But often the opposite is true!)

At this point the soul seems cast off and experiences nothing of the Lord but indignation. Now where does this believer look for help at such a time? There are two choices. One is to turn toward the Lord and the other one is to look at the temptations, the wretchedness, the poverty, the imperfections.

In the beginning of the spiritual adventure we often see the soul suffering persecution with *calmness* and *resolution*. Where does he find such reserve? He is clearly aware and keenly conscious that what is happening to him is *undeserved*. But in the case which I have just described *that is no longer true*! On *this* dark night he really feels that what is happening to him is his just dessert; and added to it are inexplicable confusions and humiliations. All this serves to point out to this one his need of Christ, the need of being detached from things of this creation and even from spiritual enjoyment — and to realize *what he really is, apart* from Christ's grace! Unbeknown to him, despite the ties of this earth, the heavy weights, the throes of agony which sweep over him a thousand times a day, and the sense that God has moved away to some other universe . . . he is progressing!

Vol. Page 201

# 13

# ONLY A FEW TOUCH
# THIS EXPERIENCE

This Christian has deeply loved his Lord, but now all things of his interior life seem to be dissolved. He is forced to abandon the precious solitude he has enjoyed. Strength is gone. Grace is gone. He despairs of himself. He hates that which he sees of himself and is resolved to have no more to do with trusting in his nature. He expects nothing from himself and begins to wait upon God, *the God who is not there*, knowing that he must trust in *this* Lord.

Do not think that these kinds of experiences will ever come in the same way to those who are unconverted or those who follow an external walk. They simply cannot feel such deep pains, for they are quenching the revelation of the Holy Spirit in such matters. I am speaking, then, of those who, having been tempted, proven and tried, are deemed worthy to undergo such experiences. They are deemed worthy only because of the fact they have an element of *unconscious* fidelity toward their Lord *and* a deep humility. They *do not* perceive either of these elements within themselves.

# 14

# REBELLION
# WHICH MAY NOT BE REBELLION

There is a word of comfort I would bring here.

It is important to bear in mind that there are two ways to resist God. One is voluntary and willful. This kind of resistance stops the work of God. Your Lord cannot violate man's freedom of will. But there is also a resistance that can be called "the resistance of nature." This resistance lies in the will, but it is there without being voluntary. I speak simply of the human tendency of repugnance toward one's own destruction, the instinct of survival. Without seeking to measure the depth of this repugnance or to evaluate this natural rebellion against our own annihilation, we recognize that God relates to this type of resistance in a totally different way than He does rebellion.

In the face of this resistance, the Lord does not cease

His effectual working; rather He seeks to take advantage of a true consecration which this believer once made to his Lord and to himself: a willingness toward *total abandonment*, a willingness which has never been withdrawn and which is not now withdrawn. The will itself *has* remained submissive, perhaps even subdued, to God despite the rebellion that is found in the feelings.

This abandonment and this submission of the will is concealed — somewhere in the very depths of the soul — and is often not recognized by the Christian . . . but seen only by God. I have called this "the passage of the hand of God."

Here is something deep within us which only God can see, and having seen it, He is able to continue His purifying operation in us without violating our freedom.

# 15

# GOD'S PLAN

When I speak of God unfolding His plan in detail, I do not mean that God says to the soul of the believer, "In order for you to know exactly what to renounce and what to sacrifice, you must do this and this and this."

No. Not at all! There is but one way God explains His design for your life. It is this: He does it by putting the soul of the believer into the crucible of the most severe trials. He brings that soul to the point of sacrificing to his Lord all that he possesses, and not only what he possesses but his entire being, and not just for time only, but for all eternity.

How is such a sacrifice accomplished? One writer of the interior way said the only way we will ever come to such a sacrifice is by "the soul's absolute despair of itself." This has been called the *holy* despair. Despair must become so intense that every support in the individual is taken away and he is forced into an unconditional abandonment of himself into the hands of God.

Most Christians do not know what it means to despair of themselves. Few people *ever* know the utter limits of that despair . . . the *despair* of all *despairs*, when you come to know *exactly* what you really are.

It is a terrible, devastating thing to discover what you really are.

You must remember this: The more you despair of self, the more you *trust in God*. You can be sure that you do not always recognize the second part of that truth . . . that of having *trusted in God*. Nonetheless, it is true. The further removed you are from certainty, the further you are also removed from a faith which rests on sight, and the more deeply you enter into faith in God.

This comes when you are stripped of every support. Whenever God takes away anything from the believer's soul, it is sacrifice. But what is the last sacrifice of all? It is the one that I describe as "the pure sacrifice." Sacrifice made by the willing soul of the believer.

This ultimate sacrifice might be described thus: The believer has abandoned his soul to God. He has abandoned his self-nature and he has abandoned the things of the creature, only to discover that he has been abandoned *by* God. At this discovery, the Christian cries out to his God, "Oh God, why have you forsaken me!" (The entire and absolute sacrifice of Jesus Christ can be found in the words, "My God, why hast thou forsaken me?" and "Into your hands I commend my spirit.") It is this surrender of the whole self, for all time and eternity, which is given up to God. *This* is, in fact, the *last sacrifice*. The cry which comes after that, "It is finished," announces the completion of the soul's sacrifice.

All of our troubles spring from our resistance; and our resistance comes from our attachment to things. The more you torment yourself over your suffering, the sharper that suffering becomes. But if you surrender yourself to suffering, more each time, and if you allow the crucifying process to go on undisturbed, the suffering is used more effectively.

Do not come to this immature idea: "I will be one of those who constantly follows His will, and I will *always* surrender to suffering; *then* He will not find it necessary to deal with me so harshly."

There is no such person. There is no such possibility! There never will be. Self is great in all of us. And the revelation of our true nature is shocking. We all must know unbelievable, almost unbearable suffering. Nor can *you* seek and find *your* weaknesses and quickly deal with them. Your arrogance only shows itself, your pride betrays itself, when you entertain such thoughts!

The soul becomes acquainted with its hindrances only *after* those hindrances are removed.

4th chapter
Vol. II
Page 207

# 16

# WHEN REVELATION
# PRECEDES SUFFERING

In the Song Of Songs, Chapter 5, you find a reference to two kinds of resistance of which the soul is capable. The voice of the groom calls to his spouse, "Open to me, for I am heavy with the drops of love."

Here the soul sees clearly that the Lord who has come is a Lord loaded down with grief. He has come to make her a partaker of His suffering. As He speaks there is the evidence of pain. She senses this. She understands it is a grief almost indescribable. If she could be strong in her suffering, she would bear that grief gladly.

The one speaking to her lets her know she will suffer not only physical pain but the loss of reputation, and will know persecution by slander. And so it comes to pass.

Why does He do this to her? So that she might learn

the absolutely innumerable frailties which she has, and to help her to understand her wretchedness. The only way this is possible is by a loss of strength and virtue toward resisting those things that are actually repugnant to her. Yes, and the loss of the ability to do good works. She is covered with an inconceivable confusion. She suffers great distress.

He delivers the external part of her being to many calamities and to the maliciousness of man and even to the powers of darkness. It appears that He has given each of these attackers an unrestricted power over her external nature. Furthermore, the Lord lays His hand heavily upon her interior nature.

Even the thought of such things makes one shudder! While the believer passes through this trial, he probably feels extreme rebellion against the suffering. He looks about for some trace of abandonment he once had toward his Lord. There is nothing there — neither without nor within. He cries from deep within his inmost being for strength or for deliverance. It seems that *neither* comes.

Interestingly, just before these things happen in the lives of many believers, there is actually a *revelation*. Perhaps we should call it an *infusion* of divine justice. There comes a sense that whatever the Lord does in our lives, *it is just*! The believer realizes that, whether it be an attack from the powers of darkness, or simply His own natural weakness exposed . . . *whatever* is about to befall him, it is justified. He is being prepared for something.

He is being prepared to face what is before him without reservation and without any distinct view in mind as to what the outcome will be. He has been given the ability to surrender to whatever it is the Lord is about to do. (This does not guarantee his survival; it only guarantees that he has given God unlimited access to do, at His full power and sovereign will, whatever He decides to do.)

In such a moment of calamity, that previous revelation of divine justice is often not there. But on other occasions — in the very depths of all of this calamity — a sense, an apprehension, and yes, even a love of divine justice does return. And when that happens, the soul of the believer cannot refrain itself! Once more that Christian will renew his sacrifice at the altar of the Lord.

Be assured, though, when the tempest reaches the apex of its fury, once more the thoughts of such consecration vanish; the awareness of devotion to the Lord passes away. The believer forgets his sacrifice and his love of justice; he is simply overwhelmed by the repugnance of what is happening. He knows only an experience of the pains of death.

There are other things which may happen just before one is plunged into such trials. On some occasions God will set before the soul of that believer an understanding of what suffering is . . . and then request that the believer consent to what is about to take place.

Some refuse. Some simply are not able to yield to known sacrifice. Some refuse absolutely; others will take a few days before they can render up that sacrifice. In every case, the resistance to what has been placed before them comes with great torment, especially to that believer who has in previous times been yielding and obedient. (That believer may very well be facing the fact that God is exposing a secret pride which has developed in him because he has been faithful in the past!) He knows that in the past he has never refused anything from the hand of God, no matter how exacting His demands; yet his resistance, based on a new and deeper comprehension of the cross, of suffering and of the self-nature, leaves him in a place where surrender to this coming holocaust is virtually impossible.

*The Lord allows us to resist the sacrifice and the cross.* There is a reason for the resistance. It is the same one the girl felt in the Song Of Songs. She was filled with repugnance at receiving a groom who was covered with blood and who had come steeped in such great grief. But the believer does not, and must not, resist for a long period of time. The resistance is necessary. We might even say that it is *good*, for it convinces the believer of his frailty and proves to him how far he is from possessing the courage he so fondly imagined he had.

What is true of him is also true of you and *all* of us. There simply is no such thing in any of our lives. If we perceive that we are so endowed, we are but fooling ourselves.

The young maiden in the Song Of Songs has just known a wonderful and pure experience of the delights of mutual love, given and received, between herself and her Lord. Now suddenly she finds herself very weak when love comes, making its demands in the form of crucifixion.

Why this change in attitude? Perhaps it is because this one, having previously been faithful, experiences great pain at seeing the demands of crucifixion and wonders at its purpose and its necessity. Again, the knowledge of your weakness, even after wonderful spiritual experience with your Lord . . . the knowledge of just how weak you really are, when faced with a cross and with suffering, is very revealing; and in that knowledge itself is great pain and suffering.

Vol. II
Page 208

# 17

# THE OPENING OF THE SOUL
# TO THE GROOM

In Chapter 5 of the Song Of Songs (verse 6) the believing one does open her heart to her beloved; from this new opening of the soul, there comes a renewed abandonment. Resistance has been laid aside. The soul makes a new, expressed act of surrender and abandonment to the Lord.

Once a soul has been unfaithful —or resistant —the Lord will always return to extract just such a demand, so that the believing one may renew, and return to, his onward course with the Lord.

# 18

# THERE IS ONLY ONE TRUE
# RIGHTEOUSNESS

A trial is set before a Christian. Along with this trial is the experience and revelation which this person is going through by seeing his own wretchedness. He finds himself stripped of all support. There is nothing of his own righteousness to hold him up. (I stress the point, *his own* righteousness.) It is good that this Christian knows that there is no righteousness and fidelity which has any real merit in his own life.

Why?

To appropriate the things of God to your nature (that is, to think that the things which are characteristic of God are also characteristics of yours), *this* must pass away! There must come that moment when the believer confesses that all righteousness belongs to God alone, that *nothing* is righteous outside of Him. One must come to that point where he has become so weak and so unstable in his own view of himself that he has no recourse left to him but to trust only in the righteousness of God. He recognizes God's all and his own nothingness; God's omnipotence and his own weakness. He is soon, therefore, established in an abandonment that is rarely, if ever, shaken thereafter.

Vol. II
Page 115

# 19

# FIRE HAS ITS CONDITIONS

When a fire reaches the forest, it blackens the wood before it burns the wood. So also is the approach of fire as it closes in upon the soul. The fire blackens the soul before it burns the soul. Dryness in wood is necessary for its burning. And blackening always preceeds burning.

Wood may also be discolored by moisture; but if there is wetness, the wood is not fit to be burned. In fact, wood can become so wet that it will not burn at all.

Such is the blackness of those who depart from You, oh God! Such are those who go forth into adultery with the world (Psalm 73:27).

Such ones shall perish, but not so the soul that is rendered dark-complected in the way recorded in the Song Of Songs (Chapter 1).

*You*, oh God, will cleanse from her everything opposed

to your purity. You take away the water and render her dry.

When *You* love, *your* love is *always* excessive. Your love is intended to perfect us . . . in yourself. You show us that we are dark-complected before You consume us.

# 20

# DARKNESS AND GOD'S PRESENCE

John Of the Cross speaks of several purgings that the spiritual pilgrim passes through on his way to the depths of God. He calls the first stage *the night of the senses*. He calls the very *last* stage *the night of the Spirit*. It is in this last state that your God communicates Himself to the soul of the believer in a way that is far more perfect than He does in any other stage through which the soul will pass.

Here is something you cannot be convinced of, and it is something which cannot be explained. It is, nonetheless, the truth.

The greater the purity of a dark night of the spirit, the greater the sublimity of the manifestation of that night. The more terrible the absence of the groom, the more complete, the greater the purification.

The measure of His hiding from you seems to match the measure of His revelation.

These ultimate trials (the experience of the night of the spirit) become even more agonizing than others because, in addition to the absence of the groom, the believer's soul is overwhelmed with a deep conviction of his own wretchedness. There is distress in this, and usually — almost always — there is an accompanying persecution from men. (It seems as if it is from devils.)

You cannot come to an idea of this terrible tribulation except by having passed through the actual experience.

The Lord's hiding from the believer's spirit is well termed a *night* and a *death*.

Your Lord is the light and your Lord is the life of your soul. Therefore it seems when the light goes out the soul is in terror. But there is another way for you to consider this thing called *the dark night*; and that is to realize that when light is intensely bright, it shows objects to be far more horrible and more terrifying than they were when they were in the dark. Look upon the dark night of the spirit as a terrible revealing of the truth of what you are. And as you pass through this inexplicable experience, and when you have lost all hope of ever beholding another dawn, remember that to Him *even darkness is light*.

Vol. II
Page 276

# 21

# INWARD WOUNDS
# AND OUTWARD WOUNDS

There are wounds that are inflicted upon you at the discretion of your Lord. These are the agonies of the soul and they are *inward*. But there are also wounds that are *without* . . . persecution, malice and those things inflicted by man and by the realm of darkness. There must be wounds from within and wounds from without.

We have been speaking of a dark night of the spirit, an apparent loss of the Lord's presence. The spouse, during this time, is not occupied with self nor with other creatures. She *is*, in fact, further away from being unfaithful than any other time in her experience. (This does not mean that she knows this.) Actually, she thinks she has *lost* the presence of her well-beloved, and she continually grieves at this seemingly perpetual absence of her Lord.

What she does not know is that there is, deep within her, an interior eye which is turned toward God and is unfailingly preserved — though she is not conscious of it. The spouse never forgets her groom. The absence of her Lord is so all-consuming, she loses attention to herself without even realizing it. And though she feels her Lord is gone, her heart is applied toward Him. She has not put Him out of her mind because *His absence is constantly* there to remind her of Him.

This is so totally unlike those who forced Him out of their mind so that they could return to sin without restraint.

Upon her awakening, she will learn a most valuable lesson: That sense of void, that sense of nothingness, that sense of lostness, that sense of being forsaken and abandoned by God . . . that powerful, ceaseless sense which is with the interior believer day and night, awake or asleep . . . even *this* is Christ!

Vol. II
Page 282 and 283

# 22

# PERSECUTION FROM FOUR SOURCES

There are those who seek to serve their Lord. It is common, at the very beginning of this serving, to experience persecution at the hands of the ungodly. But the more such a Christian is persecuted, the more he seems to discover those around him who share this common interest in serving Christ.

This is not so with those who devote themselves to the interior life. They suffer persecution at the hands of the *godless world*, but they also receive persecution from *people who live ordinary lives*; and, even more, they suffer from pious and *religious-minded* men and women who are *not interior.*

It is the religious-minded who persecute as a matter of duty! In our day and the ages preceding us, and perhaps in whatever years lie ahead, the pattern is the same. People are not able to recognize any other way as right except the one that they are walking.

But the most violent assaults that the interior Christian will know come from Christians who *pretend* — the ones who have a devotion to God, a *false* devotion. There is a foul character within these people, a wickedness and hypocrisy. The internal one recognizes this, and in some way this recognition provokes hostility from those who *oppose* the interior way. It seems almost like a conflict between angels and devils.

Vol. III
Page 55

# 23

# THE JEALOUSY OF GOD

The Lord is jealous. But why?

One reason is because there is such a small number of those who consecrate themselves to Him without any reservation. They are so few, He does not allow for a rival. Therefore, He takes little delight in divided souls. Those who are entirely devoted to Him, He loves; and He regards them as His own peculiar property. He exercises all His rights over them. (He does this without interfering with their freedom of will. After all, their abandonment is open and is hearty and is perfectly voluntary.) Nonetheless, He has a jealousy for this kind of believer. He cannot abide the flaws that are in them. They are His choice, and are locked up in the inmost part of His heart. There is another curiosity here, too. *He does not often allow them to be seen by the curious gaze* of an unappreciating world. They are mostly hidden ones.

# 24

# THE TRUE EMPLOYMENT OF MAN'S FREE WILL

God has a tendency to reunite Himself with the believer. Every moment of your life, God is shedding His infinite love and benevolence upon you and upon every human soul. It is natural to His being to communicate. He *must* necessarily communicate Himself to every person who is disposed to receive His gifts. As the dew falls upon every object that is exposed to the sky, so He is incessantly communicating Himself to you.

However, when He created man He created man *free*. Man, therefore, has the power of shutting himself up — yes, even sheltering himself from the celestial dew of heaven. Man can turn his back upon God. He can lay hindrance upon hindrance in the path of his Lord for, if he does not, he *shall be reached* by God's mercy.

Man *will find* his God *unless* he deliberately shuts doors!

What effect, then, is there when a man begins to remove some of those barriers which he has put in the way? He is induced to turn toward the source, even his Lord. After all, who could not turn when, unceasingly, love rains upon the heart.

No sooner is the heart turned, and opened a little, than the dew of His grace comes falling gently into that heart. And according to the amount of the love that falls, so is the growth of love in that heart toward the Lord. And the more widely that person is open to God, the more profuse is the fall of the dew.

There is something you must remember: Love prepares His own way. No one else can prepare the way for the Lord except the Lord Himself. He prepares your heart and leads your heart from fullness to fullness. He is the one who enlarges; and as He enlarges, He fills.

Your Lord abhors an empty heart.

It is true that it seems sometimes He reduces the soul to emptiness and nakedness, but the desolation is only external. It is only an *appearance* of desolation. Surely it is true that He is thrusting *out* everything that is not God. But remember, just as God is love, so He can only permit Himself—and nothing else—into the soul of the man. All else that is in that soul is offensive to Him, and must be vanquished. Therefore, He sets in motion the means to purify this creature, enlarge the soul and extend—and magnify—in order that He may have room enough to dwell therein!

\* \* \* \* \*

Oh Holy Love, my Lord, where are the hearts that will submit to be thus purified? Who will allow himself to be enlarged and extended by your hand? Your operations in us seem harsh *only* because we are impure. Open our eyes to see that You are always gentle and tenderhearted.

It is a wonderful thing when a soul will open his heart to You and allow your admission, even if he does it with the greatest of hesitation.

How straightened You are in such hearts. What confined quarters, what an unclean residence is found therein for the infinite God of purity.

Oh, Love, our Lord, are You not power? Must we make no other use of our liberty but to resist Thee? Oh, what a sad *gift* it is which we employ, the *ability* to resist You!

Oh, freedom of will, oh, gift, your only *true employment* is the sacrificing of yourself to your Lord.

Our only true employment, oh, God, is in sacrificing all to Thee.

Vol. III
Page 109

# 25

# THE CONSUMMATION
# OF THE INTERIOR LIFE

Most of those who have spoken on the interior way speak of its consummation in the next life. When I think of the next world in relationship to the interior life, I too, see an experience of the consummation of grace and glory. And, yes I see a completion of all increase and merit . . . the fruit and the recompense and the unclouded enjoyment of the truth of those things which are deep within us. But as to the interior life itself, I see that life completed in the perfect proportion— and in final proportion —while still here in this present life.

After all, the interior life is *begun* here — is begun with a redemption that is perfect in every sense. The *progress* of the interior life is *here*; that hunger of always seeking after God is *here* (a hunger that avoids and flees from everything contrary to Him and is purified from everything contrary to Him).

The *end* of the interior life is also here on this earth. I would qualify that by saying that I speak of the *state* of rest, and the *state* of satisfaction in the Sovereign Good. This state of rest, in God, has been the object of the soul's desire from the moment of its first seeking to know Him.

When I speak of the *completion*, (that is, the *maturity*) of the interior life in this lifetime, it must be remembered that this does not impede further progress in God in the life to come. The state may be perfected here (that is, as far as the *action* of the *creature* is concerned) but, of course, it is *truly* finished *only* in relationship to the perfecting hand of God.

I would like to illustrate with the human body how this matter appears to me.

We call a body *complete* when it has all of its members. Now all around us are those who are lame and blind and maimed. The members of their body are *present*, but they are not mature *and* not complete. There is the difference. We seek after a physical body that is mature and that is *proportioned* in every way, a body which possesses the *full use* of all its members.

Beyond this maturity, though, there is another form and another beauty. And what is that? When the the body is not only complete in its members and mature in its members but *also* when each separate member has full proportion, color and *harmony* in relationship to a matured, harmonious, perfectly formed body.

When there is beauty, harmony and proportion, then we think of the body as being complete and mature, *both* in its parts and in its *whole*. (I do not deny that this is nothing to be compared with the perfection that will come with *glorification* of the human body. The present maturity of a body is not to be compared with that body which is risen and stands in the state of glory.)

I see, then, a fully mature interior life in the same way. In the life to come we will, of course, enjoy a totally different perfection as the mortality puts on immortality, and even the body becomes a spiritual entity.

Nonetheless, there is a maturity for here and now, for each part to be complete and whole, for each part to be mature, and for all parts to be in harmony with all the other parts, thereby making a *whole* which is perfectly mature in growth, in proportion, in beauty and in harmony.

# SHORT
# SELECTIONS
# FROM
# JUSTIFICATIONS

# SHORT SELECTIONS

Perfect love does not know what it is to consider self-interest.

◆ ◆ ◆

To rob God of nothing . . . to refuse nothing . . . to require of Him nothing . . . this is great perfection.

◆ ◆ ◆

There are many who are content to bear the cross, but there is scarcely a single one who is willing to bear the infamy.

◆ ◆ ◆

When the heart of a man displays significant fidelity to be willing to give up all the gifts of God in order that he may reach God himself, then it is that God takes great pleasure in showering upon that one a profusion of the very gifts which he did not seek.

◆  ◆  ◆

The soul which has found its center becomes so strong that it has nothing further to fear from that which is without.

◆  ◆  ◆

The ongoing purpose of *union* is to strengthen the soul so fully that it no longer suffers those faintings which beset the beginner, who, grace being so feeble in him, experiences eclipses and falls.

◆  ◆  ◆

An external cross is a small matter *if* unaccompanied by a cross which is *internal*. The inward cross renders *much more* painful the simultaneous presence of an outward cross.

◆  ◆  ◆

The believer perceives nothing but the cross on every side. That cross is nevertheless nothing more than the Beloved Himself in the shape of a cross. Your Lord is never more present to you than in those seasons of bitterness.

During those times He dwells in the very midst of your heart.

◆ ◆ ◆

The Lord often permits the humble exterior of one He has chosen, to offend others . . . even those who are partakers of the graces of that believer. Consequently, those who are partakers of that Christian's graces often separate themselves from him after God has produced the effect that He wanted in their lives through the means of that chosen one.

◆ ◆ ◆

There are some things about our Lord and His ways that can only be deemed worthy by declaring them to be above and beyond all praise.

◆ ◆ ◆

All the operations of God in your interior are toward two things: One is to deliver the soul from wickedness and from the malignity of its fallen nature. The second is to restore the interior — the soul itself — to God; to restore it, as fair and pure as can be rendered this side of the fall.

◆ ◆ ◆

I have noticed that advanced souls frequently

experience something rather surprising. It is this. During the night, while they are more or less asleep, God seems to operate more powerfully than during the day!

◆  ◆  ◆

In the soul that watches for its God even though its exterior is dead, stunned and benumbed, like a body that is in deep sleep, there is still the constancy of the heart retaining a secret and hidden vigor which preserves that soul's oneness with God.

◆  ◆  ◆

To that believer who has reached God, there is no longer any winter. There is a season composed of the other three seasons joined together as one. Having reached an *inner-winter* the soul passes through all the seasons of the spiritual life. Afterwards it re-enters into a perpetual season that is a spring, a summer, and an autumn combined. The mildness of spring does not prevent the fervor of summer nor the fruitfulness of autumn; the heat of summer does not interfere with the beauty of spring nor the abundance of the autumn; and the fruits of the autumn interpose no obstacle to the enjoyment of spring nor the ardor of summer.

Oh, happy land. Happy are they who are enabled to possess you.

◆  ◆  ◆

If a Christian dare aspire to a touch of union with the divine he must be well persuaded of the all of God and his own nothingness. He must go forth feeling nothing but contempt and hatred for his self-nature and reserve all his esteem and all of his love for God. By this means he may attain to that union.

* * *

As God reigns *in* Jesus Christ, in the same way, Christ reigns *in* pure hearts. There He finds nothing that either resists or is offensive to Him. This inner place is a kingdom to us and makes us partakers of His royal estate. As the Father has appointed the Lord Jesus a kingdom, and He shares the glory of that kingdom with His Son, so His Son shares that state with us.

* * *

When the soul is perfected, or matured, in a oneness which can no more be interrupted by things that happen on the outside, the mouth of the believer is imbued with the praise appropriate to that state. The beautiful harmony between the silent word of the soul and the sensible speech of the body constitute the maturity of praise.

At this present time there are those who are martyrs, but to the Holy Spirit. I mean there are those who suffer for proclaiming the truth that the reign of the Holy Spirit in the souls of men has begun . . . and especially for proclaiming their personal and their total dependence on His divine presence and His influence. This is the doctrine of pure love, the doctrine of sanctification and of the Holy Spirit indwelling us. He is the life of our own life.

◆ ◆ ◆

Those believers who follow the will of God blindly are used to assist others into an interior path. You see, having nothing more to lose and having no longer any anxiety in regard to themselves, God can use such a person to bring others into the way of His will. Those who are still possessing much of the self could not be used for this purpose, of course.

When I say *withholding nothing*, I mean they withhold nothing which God desires in that present moment. He frequently does not permit us to point out to another believer all the things that is hindering that believer in his walk. We only speak to him in general terms because he can bear no more.

And though we may sometimes speak hard things, as Christ did to the Capernaites, the Lord, nevertheless, bestows a strength on the bearer to bear it.

◆ ◆ ◆

There are some souls who cause me great suffering. They are selfish souls who are full of compromise and speculations and desire others to accommodate them and their inclinations. I find myself unable to administer anything to them because of their self love. When I try, a hand more powerful than myself restrains me. I cannot give such a person any more place in my heart than God gives them. I cannot adapt to their superficial state nor can I respond to their profession of friendship. They are repulsive to my feelings.

The love which dwells in my heart is not a natural love. It arises from a depth which rejects what is not in correspondence with it. That is, what is not in unison with the heart of God.

I cannot be with a child without caressing it, nor with a child-like soul without tender attachment. I do not regard the external person but — rather — the state of the soul, its affinity with God and its inclination of oneness with God. The only perfect union is the union of the soul in God. Such is the arrangement in heaven and on earth after the life of the resurrection takes its full strength in the believer's soul.

◆ ◆ ◆

A shadow is never greater nor deeper than when light is at its weakest. So are those believers never greater in their own eyes than when they are smallest before God.

◆ ◆ ◆

The interior life and the oneness of the human will with the Lord's will, this is an area into which people should not intrude. That is, none should go there but those whom God calls, having, by His Spirit, prepared them. But this creates a problem. Those who have been ravenous for the first fruits of divine union — and then have such an experience with the Lord of all — feel a strong desire to share this grace with everybody else and to make their experience abundantly known. What this person does not realize is that he is taking a small grace and distributing it to everyone when it was given privately and personally for him alone; such a believer has passed out too freely the Holy oil poured into his own lamp. He will soon find that there is nothing left. The wise will watchfully keep their oil until they are introduced *into* the groom's chamber. *Then* they may share their oil, because the *Lamb* is the light which illuminates them.

◆　◆　◆

Naked faith and *total abandon* can be likened unto two cherubim which cover the ark. (It is from the mercy seat that God delivers His word.) *Faith* covers the soul, hindering the soul from examining itself and seeing anything that is opposed to it. *Abandon* hides that soul on yet another side, preventing it from regarding itself, from seeing its own loss or its own advantage, thereby obliging it to abandon itself blindly to God.

But *faith* and *abandon* look upon *each other* as did the two cherubim upon the cover of the ark. The one cannot exist without the other, so both are needed in a well-regulated soul. *Faith* perfectly responds to *abandon* when abandon is submitted to faith.

# Additional
# Selections

# ADDITIONAL SELECTIONS.

### ALL RESTORED AGAIN.

"I look upon Job's experience," says Madam Guyon, "as a mirror of the whole spiritual life." God strips him of his goods, which are gifts and graces; then of his children, which is stripping him of his faculties or good works, these being our offspring and our dearest productions; next He takes his health from him, by which is meant the loss of the virtues; then He makes him to putrify, rendering him an object of horror, of infection, and of contempt; it seems even, as if this holy man committed faults, and that he was deficient in resignation. He is accused by his friends of being justly punished by reason of his transgressions; there remains no sound part in him. But after he has rotted on the dunghill, and there remains nothing but his bones, and he is a mere corpse, God gives him back everything, goods, children, health and life."

"It is the same with those who have been crucified and buried with Christ, after they are resurrected unto newness of life; all is given back, together with an admirable facility in making use of them, without incurring the defilement, without attaching one's self to them, and without appropriating them as formerly. All is done in God, divinely, using things as not using them. In this state there is true LIBERTY and true LIFE. "If ye have been like to Jesus Christ in His death, you shall be like Him in His resurrection" (Rom. 6: 5). Is it being free to be under inability and restrictions? Nay. "If the Son shall make you free, ye shall be free indeed" (Jno. 8: 36), but free with His own liberty."

---

## DESTROYED AND RUINED.

In commenting on these words of Job, "He has destroyed me on all sides, and

I am ruined; He has taken away from me all hope, like a tree which is plucked up by the roots," Madam Guyon says: "The means of reducing a soul to total ruin, is to take from it all support, and to destroy it on all sides; for if it found the smallest prop, or the least support, it could not be destroyed; like a person who is drowning, so long as he finds props and supports he will never drown. If a person were suspended above the sea, although it might be only by a small thread, he would never fall into it, unless the thread were broken; in like manner, so long as there is even a small place in which we are not destroyed, we are not ruined. That is why Job says that since he is destroyed on all sides, he is certainly ruined, and that the hope which he had in himself, or in anything out of God, has been not only cut off (like a tree which a person simply cuts down, which would be a small matter, for it can always spring up again), but snatched away like a tree, which is plucked up by the roots, and thus cannot spring up any more, for nothing of it remains.

This comparison of the tree is a very good one, because if there remains only a little root, it will again shoot forth; likewise, if there remains anything of the self-life in us which is not taken away, it will gradually spring up, and increase. This is why, God wishing to be very merciful to the soul, does not allow the least subsistence to remain."

------

LOVE BEGETS KNOWLEDGE.

In commenting on I John 4: 7, 8, M. Guyon says:

Whatever pains the philosophers have taken to *know* God by the effort of their intellect, they *have not known Him,* because they have not loved Him, and because all the rest of the knowledge of the most learned men of the world, who are destitute of love, is a deception. In God, love brings forth knowledge, whilst amongst the creatures, love implies acquaintance. I know that one cannot love, if one does not know Him, that is to say, if one does not know that there is a God, who deserves to be loved and adored. This knowledge alone suffices to make us tend to love Him, and we no sooner love Him than we begin to have a real knowledge of what He is and of what He deserves; it is a knowledge by experience, which is only given by love; just as he who possesses a property knows infinitely better what it is worth than he who has merely heard of it. That is why it is written, "Taste and thou wilt see"—taste in the first place, by love, how lovable God is, and then *you will see,* by the knowledge which will be given to you in loving. Oh, how mistaken are those who make all piety consist in the effort of their minds to know an incomprehensible object, and who persuade themselves that prayer should be a continual reasoning! Oh, no! prayer should be a continual loving.

Do you desire to make an effectual prayer? Love much and you will succeed fully. Begin your prayer with acts and movements of love towards this God, who is all love, and not by reasonings, which, amusing your intelligence, leave

your will without nourishment; which
may be truly described as eating with
an empty mouth. Continue your prayer
by love, giving opportunity to the Well-
Beloved to communicate himself to you,
by degrees, as you try by your affection
to approach Him, and at the end finish
your prayer by a real love, and by a
desire to love always more fully this
Divine Object, who deserves all our love.
But what am I saying? "finish" your
prayer? No, my brethren, never finish
it; never cease for a moment to love,
and you will never cease to pray. The
knowledge of God should come by love,
and not by sight or study. God only
gives knowledge of Himself by His love;
he who loves the most, knows the most.

Knowledge, then, is communicated
through love: it is God's love expressed
in and by us, which moves God to discover Himself to us, to reveal Himself
in us, as Jesus Christ said. Now, as we
can only know God in such degree as
He manifests Himself to us, and as he
only manifests Himself in proportion to
our love, it is clear that he who loves the

best is he who knows the most, through love.

St. Paul says (Rom. 1 : 18-22), that there are men who have tried to know God by their natural senses, and who, knowing Him, have not adored Him as God, and consequently have not loved Him. These sublime studies, destitute of love, have only served to make their fall deeper. This shows us that love is not born of knowledge, although implicit knowledge precedes it, but that knowledge is begot by love; although afterwards, the acquaintance which love begets increases that same love; and the augmentation of the love gives a clearer acquaintance, and so on forever; the creature through all eternity loving more, and knowing more; as new fires of love arise, new illumination is given.

Love burns, or warms, and lightens. These are two inseparable qualities of fire, to heat and lighten; but the first action of fire is to heat before it illuminates, although the same energy that generates the heat brings forth the light. If we regard the thing closely we shall see that its nature is to heat, and that it only lightens because it burns. Look at a coal which becomes hot before it becomes luminous, or rather observe that the heat precedes the light, and follows it again afterwards, so that a piece of wood thrown into the fire will not give light until it is heated. When the light ceases, the heat still remains, which shows that heat is the principle of light.

Let us love, let us burn, and we shall be enlightened, we shall have the most real knowledge. These are the proper relations of the knowledge and the love of God.

Now, this love of God produces in us the love of our neighbor, because, being children of God by love, the same love which makes us love God as our Father makes us love our neighbor as our brother.

------

## THE HIDDEN MANNA.

In writing on the subject of the "Mystical Sense of the Sacred Scriptures," M. Guyon says:

The more a man believes in the all-power of God and His love for men, the more he lets himself be conducted to God by a blind *abandon,* the more he will love purely, the more also will he be enlightened as to the truths that are contained in the mystical sense of the sacred scriptures. He will discover then with infinite joy that all interior experiences are there described in a manner simple, yet clear; he will find himself happy in meeting a Guide to pass over the Red Sea, and the frightsome desert that follows; but he will not comprehend his perfect felicity until he be arrived at the promised land, where all his past labors will appear to him as dreams. Transported with so great a happiness, he will not believe it to have been too dearly bought by all the troubles he has borne, even though he should have suffered far greater.

Of so great a people that came out of the land of Egypt, there arrived only two persons into the promised land. How comes this? From want of courage, regretting unceasingly that they had left. If they had been courageous and faithful, only a few months would have been necessary to arrive there; but murmuring and despondency made them remain on the road forty years. It happens as much thus to persons who God desires to conduct by the interior way. They grieve, not for the onions of Egypt, but for the sensible sweetness when they are asked to walk in a purer and barer road. They do not wish so delicate a food as manna, they desire something more sensible. They revolt against their leader, and far from profiting by the goodness of God, they raise His anger and kindle His fury; so they make for themselves an extremely long road, and turn around about the mountain; if they advance one step they fall back four, and the greater part do not arrive at the promised end by their own fault. Let us take courage, let us endeavor to reach the goal without ever being discouraged by the difficulties we find on our way. We have a sure Guide, who is this *Cloud* during the day, which, concealing from us the brightness of the sun, leads us more surely; we have during the darkest night of faith the *pillar of fire,* which guides us also. What is this *pillar of fire,* if not sacred love, which becomes the more glowing as faith appears the more obscure and dark? Let us be content with this hidden manna of the interior, which will nourish us much better than the grosser meats that our senses so ardently desire. Let us choose the mystic tomb and not that of *concupiscense.*

----

## LEAVE IT TO GOD.

The stripping of the soul must be left to God. He will do it to perfection, while the soul will second this stripping and the whole process of death without interposing any obstacle. But to do it of one's self is to spoil all, and make of a divine, a common state. Thus you see some who, from having read or heard that the soul must be stripped of all, set about it themselves, and continue always thus without progress; for as they strip their own selves, God does not clothe them with Himself; for, it must be observed, the Divine purpose in unclothing is only to clothe upon. He impoverishes only to make rich, becoming in secret Himself the substitute for all that He takes away from the soul. This is not the case with those who act in this matter from themselves. They lose, indeed, by their faults the gifts of God; but they do not, for all that, possess God.

---

## DRIVEN INTO THE DESERT.

In commenting upon the words of Leviticus 16: 9, 10: "He shall offer a sin offering of the goat on which the lot fell. But the goat on which the lot fell for the scape-goat, he shall present living before the Lord, to offer prayers upon him, and to send him away into the desert," Madam Guyon says:

There are two kinds of deserts; the first relates to ourselves, and through which we must pass before being able to aid others—the desert of ourselves—this separation and division from all things and ourselves by dying to and renouncing everything—by quitting ourselves so absolutely that we no more take part in what regards us, than if we existed no longer—leaving ourselves destitute in God's hands, and lost in Him for time and eternity.

The other desert is that to which the Apostolic man is often banished for his brother's sake. He must bear his weaknesses, be exiled, so to speak, from God, on account of him, bear his different dispositions, be driven into the desert; for he has been made as a scape-goat for his brethren; and this is an extension of the mission of Jesus, and of the Apostolic life.

The lots cast upon the two goats, and the destination made of them by the Lord, mark that all purified souls are not called to the Apostolic life. These two goats represent two kinds of persons, called of God to be offered up to

Him by different sacrifices. Some by
the loss of themselves into God, pecu-
liarly belong to Him, and He destines
them to the most eminent grace, which
is, to be reserved for Him alone, and to
be sacrificed to Him without reserve and
without there remaining to them any
means of preservation. Others are des-
tined for good works—for holy activities, and finish their life thus and holily,
and receive their reward of God.

---

## THE WAY, TRUTH AND LIFE.

In commenting on the words: "I am
the way, and the truth, and the life; no
man cometh unto the Father but by me"
(John 14: 6), Madam Guyon says: It is
I, said Jesus Christ, who am the Way,
leading you. I will not let you go
astray. It is necessary that every one
walk in this way, for no one can follow
after me except by living as I have lived.

And when one shall have walked in
this Way, they will enter into the Truth,
unto which this Way leads. I am, myself, this Truth. As *man,* I am the Way

that he must follow; as *Word,* I am the Truth which teaches him who listens to it, and who loses himself in this same Truth. And why should I not be the Truth; I who am the true expression of my Father? Being the End where all His knowledge terminates, I must necessarily be His Light, and His Truth.

Therefore, in following the human life of Jesus Christ, we enter into His Truth by the Word. But how do we enter there? By listening to Him as the Father has instructed us, namely: This is my well-beloved Son, whom I have begotten by the Way of knowledge; listen to Him!

He is the Truth who can speak only of God. Oh, how beneficial it is to listen to this Divine Word, and to enter into His Truth. The heart of man is made in an admirable manner to receive this Truth of the Word, which is none other than His Spirit. It has two little ears, whose movements are wholly His, as if He said: I must not move except to listen. But in proportion as it opens one ear to receive it closes the other, to signify that if it opens to this Word it must be closed to all the rest. And also, when it has received, it closes itself in order to preserve this Spirit in it; but it opens again, at the same time, in order to send back this Spirit to Him who has communicated it. This is the office of the heart of man, whose one duty is to listen to the Word which is sent.

After the soul has walked in the Way of Jesus Christ—as man, and has entered into Jesus Christ as the Truth—the Word, it receives afterwards a new inflowing of His life. Then He forms Himself in the soul, is, so to speak, *incarnated* there; and it is then, after having followed Jesus Christ—as man and entering into His Truth—the Word, He comes in to give *Life* to it in His state of man-God; giving a life humanly-divine and divinely-human to the soul in which only He lives, and which has no more of its own life.

All this must be taken in the mystical sense, as it has been said so many times. Nevertheless, it is impossible ever to reach the Father except by the Son; and without having followed Him, at least, as the Way, we cannot be saved.

———

## TABOR, THEN CALVARY.

Commenting on the words: "Then answered Peter, and said unto Jesus, Lord, it is good for us to be here; if thou wilt let us make here three tabernacles; one for Thee, and one for Moses, and one for Elias" (Matt. 17: 4), Madam Guyon says:

Jesus chose three apostles to be witnesses of His glory, in order to strengthen them to endure future sufferings; and that they might be steadfast at the time of His passion; that they might not be offended at His ignominious death. At the same time He transports them in spirit to God, where He gives to them the knowledge of the life of the Word; for it is not to be supposed that He revealed to them the glory of His *humanity* by a privilege so singular, without exalting them to some deep knowledge of His *divinity*.

Up to that time they were well satisfied that Jesus was the Son of God, and the true God, by the special revelation which had been made to them, and by the public confession which Peter made of it. But these three disciples, so favored, received a deeper knowledge of the Life of the Word in the Father, and of the Father in the Word, which is well expressed for a short time, by the brightness of the face of Jesus Christ, and by the lustre of His raiment, which was dazzling, but which remained concealed under this new light itself.

The life of Jesus was a common life, in which there was little that was extraordinary in regard to His person. His transfiguration was a phenomenon by which He wished to distinguish it, and a place remarkable by the reflection that was made *without* of the glory that was hidden *within.*

When a soul is advanced in God, it reflects sometimes *without,* something of that which takes place *within;* but this is rare, especially in souls of faith, who lose all, and whom God loves to keep concealed; and it is this common state that Jesus bore the most, hiding His true *nature* beneath the life of a captive; becoming like men, and appearing as other men.

Also, the transfiguration of the Saviour was of short duration, because He must live in an ordinary manner, in order that all might imitate His life, and especially to give, to those who have surrendered *all,* the example and the grace of a permanent life, which is a life of *faith* and of the *heart,* and not a life of lights and illuminations; these gifts being transitory, and graces which we ought not to desire.

But because it was necessary that Jesus Christ should sanctify all the state, He bore, also, that of the transfiguration; not only that it might be a sign of a transitory grace and of some special illumination, but also that it might be an example of the state of transformation which takes place in the soul when God causes it to pass into Himself with an unspeakable purity; and being delivered from itself, to pass into God, it loses *its form,* in order to be lost in the Divine immensity.

This takes place in the depth of the soul, which remains a long time in this Divine life and centre before the transformation of the soul goes beyond to the outward transformation, which only takes place very late; but when it takes place, *the body,* represented by the vesture of Jesus Christ, partakes of a purity wholly angelic; the soul at the same time being rendered wholly light, in the most subtle part of the spirit, even as the face of Jesus became all-brilliant with light.

This conversation of Moses and Elias with Jesus was a resignation or abolishment of the severity of the Law, to give place to the Gospel of Grace, and a testimony that the Spirit of Jesus Christ was interior—the soul and the life of all "the Law and the Prophets." It was necessary that they should be present at this mystery, in order to show that all that took place in them and through them was only a representation or figure of that which must be accomplished in Jesus Christ, and through Him, in all pure souls.

Peter, who wished to prevent his Master from suffering, desired very much to have Him remain in His enjoyment, and to stay there with Him. How many times do we commit like infidelities, and fall into worse mistakes than those of Peter, seeking rest and life when the question is one of suffering and death; demanding the glory of Tabor, when it is necessary to go to the sacrifice of Calvary; and entertaining ourselves in the enjoyment of the peacefulness of a small gift of God, which is only given to us that we may go *beyond it,* and to create a desire to *seek God only!* A soul, not yet advanced, experiencing some communication of the glory of the Son of God, might wish to remain there always, and to establish there its rest, seeing nothing better. "Let us make here," say they, "tabernacles, in order to rest here, and to lead a tranquil life." Oh, poor, blind souls! You do not know what you demand any more than Peter knew what he was saying. The question here is concerning the cross, and not yet of enjoyment.

Peter acted here like all beginners in

the spiritual way ; he wished to keep *all,* joining the old law to the new, and uniting the austerity of Elias with the gentleness of Jesus Christ. That is inconsistent. It is necessary that one should give place to the other. These persons, in the beginning, do not yield to the Spirit of Jesus Christ, because they wish to keep all and to lose nothing.

It is only necessary to have a tabernacle for Jesus Christ ; the servants must submit to the master, and when God wishes to come Himself, all the devices and works of men must disappear. For *this* life, the tabernacle of Jesus finds more satisfaction in the crucified than in the illuminated soul.

---

## IN, OF, AND FOR GOD.

The holiness that God demands of us is a holiness relating to his own. Now, the holiness of God is in himself, of himself, and for himself ; it is therefore necessary that the holiness of these souls be *in* God, *of* God, and *for* God. It must be *in* God, existing only in him, otherwise it would be proprietary, and would rob him of something; and *of* God, seeing that all holiness that is not received from God cannot be called such; and *for* God, as it must refer to him as to its end and centre, and must serve his glory. The soul then arrived into God, has no longer anything *in* itself, *for* itself, nor *of* itself; but by its loss into God, everything is received in him alone; and that which it possesses is not for itself, any more than it comes from itself. But, as everything has come from God, so has everything flowed there again.

-------

TAKE HEED HOW YOU JUDGE.

Those who look at a tree with an evil eye account its fruits to be evil. I am said to be charged with being a hypocrite. But by what evidence is the charge supported? It is certainly a strange hypocrisy which voluntarily spends its life in suffering; which endures the cross in its various forms, the calumny, the poverty, the persecution, and every kind of affliction, without any reference to worldly advantages. I think one has never seen such hypocrisy as this before.

If such are the leading elements involved in hypocrisy, I must do myself the justice to say that I disclaim any acquaintance with it. I call God to witness that I would not have endured what it has been my lot to endure, if by so doing I could have been made empress of the whole earth, or have been canonized while living.

It was not earth, but God, that called me. I heard a Voice which I could not disobey. I desired to please God alone; and I sought Him, not for what He might give me, but only for Himself. I had rather die than do anything against His will.

This is the sentiment of my heart, a sentiment which no persecutions, no trials, have made me alter.

# THE DEEPER CHRISTIAN LIFE

Are you interested in reading more about the deeper Christian life?

If you are, let us suggest the order in which to read the following books, all of which have been written on the deep aspects of the Christian life.

By all means, begin with *The Divine Romance*. Then we recommend *Experiencing the Depths of Jesus Christ* and *Practicing His Presence*. Follow that with *Final Steps in Christian Maturity* and *The Inward Journey*.

For a study in brokenness, read *A Tale of Three Kings*, a favorite with thousands of believers all over the world.

To discover who you are in Jesus Christ, read *Turkeys and Eagles*, a masterfully told tale containing the very heart of the gospel as it pertains to living the Christian life.

The books entitled *The Spiritual Guide*, *Guyon Speaks Again* and *The Seeking Heart* all help to solidify, expand and buttress the things you will have read in the previous books.

You might also desire to read Guyon's *Song of the Bride*, thereby gaining her view of what she referred to as: "the Scripture, seen from *the interior way*."

# ARE YOU INTERESTED IN CHURCH LIFE?

Many Christians are interested in the vessel which is to contain the deeper Christian life . . . that is, the experience of church life.

We also recommend you read *Torch of the Testimony*, which recounts the awesome story of church life during the dark ages; and *Revolution* (vol. 1), which tells the story of the first twenty years of "church life" on the earth.

*Our Mission, Letters to A Devastated Christian,* and *Preventing A Church Split* were published specifically for Christians who have gone through - or are about to go through - the trauma of a church split . . . a devastating experience virtually every Christian will go through at least once. Because these three books (and *A Tale of Three Kings*) are virtually the only books written on this subject, you may wish to share these books with a friend who might need them.

Please write for further information.

# CLASSICS ON THE DEEPER CHRISTIAN LIFE

## Practicing His Presence

The monumental seventeenth century classic by Brother Lawrence, now in modern English. (One of the most read and recommended Christian books of the last 300 years.)

The twentieth century missionary, Frank Laubach, while living in the Philippines, sought to put into practice Brother Lawrence's words. Included in this edition are excerpts from Frank Laubach's diary.

## The Spiritual Guide

At the time Jeanne Guyon was teaching in the royal court of Louis XIV (in France), a man named Michael Molinos was leading a spiritual revival among the clergy and laymen of Rome! He actually lived in the Vatican, his influence reaching to all Italy and beyond. The great, near great, the unknown sought him out for spiritual counsel. He was the spiritual director of many of the illuminaries of the seventeenth century. He wrote *The Spiritual Guide* to meet the need of a growing hunger for spiritual direction. The book was, for a time, banned and condemned to be burned. The author was convicted and sentenced to a dungeon after one of the most sensational trials in European history.

Here, in modern English, is that remarkable book.

**Letters to a Devastated Christian**

Edwards writes a series of letters to a Christian devastated by the authoritarian movement, who has found himself on the edge of bitterness.

# BOOKS BY GUYON

**Experiencing the Depths of Jesus Christ**

Guyon's first and best known book. One of the most influential pieces of Christian literature ever penned on the deeper Christian life. Among the multitudes of people who have read it are: John Wesley, Adoniram Judson, Watchman Nee, Jesse Penn-Lewis, Zinzendorf, and the Quakers. A timeless piece of literature that has been on the "must read" list of Christians for 300 years.

**Final Steps in Christian Maturity**

This book could well be called volume two of Experiencing the Depths of Jesus Christ. Here is a look at the experiences a more advanced and faithful Christian might encounter in his/her walk with the Lord. Without questions, next to Experiencing the Depths, here is Jeanne Guyon's best book.

**Union With God**

Written as a companion book to Experiencing the Depths of Jesus Christ, and includes 22 of her poems.

**Song of the Bride**

This book has been popular through the centuries and

has greatly influenced several other well-known commentaries on the Song of Songs.

## Guyon Speaks Again

Here is spiritual counseling at its very best. There is a Christ-centeredness to Jeanne Guyon's counsel that is rarely, if ever, seen in Christian literature. Formerly entitled Letters of Mme. Guyon.

# OTHER BOOKS BY THE SEEDSOWERS

**Turkeys and Eagles** *by Peter Lord*

Hagen and Selin have been abandoned by their parents. But they have been adopted by a flock of turkeys. Are they eagles? Or are they turkeys? Or is it possible they are eagles that have been turkeyized? But even more important, is it possible that the greatest of all tragedies has befallen you? Are you an eagle that has been turkeyized, an eagle that does not even know he is an eagle?

This book could very well transform your life, for it has profoundly affected the thousands of Christians who have heard Peter Lord tell the story.

In the finest tradition of Christian storytelling, which dates back all the way to the Lord's parables, this masterfully told tale contains the very heart of the gospel as it pertains to living the Christian life.

## Church History

These five books bring to bear a whole new perspective on church life.

### Going to Church in the First Century

A story of church life in the first century, by Robert Banks, a professor at Fuller Seminary.

### Revolution, the Story of the Early Church

This book, by Gene Edwards, tells in a "you are there" approach, what it was like to be a Christian in the first century church, recounting the events from Pentecost to Antioch.

### THE TORCH OF THE TESTIMONY

John W. Kennedy tells the little known, almost forgotten, story of evangelical Christians during the dark ages.

### WHEN THE CHURCH WAS YOUNG

A voice from the past challenges us to a radical view of the first century Church. In simple, straightforward words, Ernest Loosley shows the difference between then and now. The utter simplicity of a Church that shook the planet is contrasted with our present day organizationalism.

### THE PASSING OF THE TORCH

Throughout the ages there have been small groups of Christians who have carried foward the torch of the Lord's testimony, which is the centrality of Jesus Christ and His Church in all things.

This book is a call to men and women in this generation to take up that torch. By James Chen.

 SeedSowers

## THE WORKS OF T. AUSTIN-SPARKS

The Centrality of Jesus Christ.............................................. 19.95
The House of God.............................................................. 29.95
Ministry........................................................................... 29.95
Service.............................................................................. 19.95

## COMFORT AND HEALING

A Tale of Three Kings *(Edwards)*.................................. 8.95
The Prisoner in the Third Cell *(Edwards)*...................... 7.95
Letters to a Devastated Christian *(Edwards)*.................. 5.95
Healing for those who have been Crucified by Christians *(Edwards)*........ 8.95
Dear Lillian *(Edwards)*.................................................. 5.95

## OTHER BOOKS ON CHURCH LIFE

Climb the Highest Mountain *(Edwards)*......................... 9.95
The Torch of the Testimony *(Kennedy)*......................... 14.95
The Passing of the Torch *(Chen)*................................... 9.95
Going to Church in the First Century *(Banks)*................ 5.95
When the Church was Young *(Loosley)*.......................... 14.95
Church Unity *(Litzman, Nee, Edwards)*......................... 14.95
Let's Return to Christian Unity *(Kurosaki)*................... 14.95

## CHRISTIAN LIVING

Final Steps in Christian Maturity *(Guyon)*.................... 12.95
The Key to Triumphant Living *(Taylor)*........................ 9.95
Turkeys and Eagles *(Lord)*............................................. 8.95
Beholding and Becoming *(Coulter)*................................ 8.95
Life's Ultimate Privilege *(Fromke)*................................ 7.00
Unto Full Stature *(Fromke)*.......................................... 7.00
All and Only *(Kilpatrick)*.............................................. 7.95
Adoration *(Kilpatrick)* .................................................. 8.95
Release of the Spirit *(Nee)* ............................................ 5.00
Bone of His Bone *(Huegel)* ........................................... 8.95
Christ as All in All *(Haller)* .......................................... 9.95

Please write or call for our current catalog:

**SeedSowers**
**P.O. Box 285**
**Sargent, GA 30275**

**800-228-2665**
**www.seedsowers.com**